T0017915

Crayola! The Secrets of the
Cool Colors
and Hot Hues

by Bonnie Williams
illustrated by Rob McClurkan

Ready-to-Read

Simon Spotlight

New York   London   Toronto   Sydney   New Delhi

SIMON SPOTLIGHT
An imprint of Simon & Schuster Children's Publishing Division
1230 Avenue of the Americas, New York, New York 10020
This Simon Spotlight edition July 2018

© 2018 Crayola, Easton, PA 18044-0431. Crayola®, Crayola Oval Logo®, Chevron Design®, and
Serpentine Design® are registered trademarks of Crayola used under license. Official Licensed Product.
All rights reserved, including the right of reproduction in whole or in part in any form.
SIMON SPOTLIGHT, READY-TO-READ, and colophon are registered trademarks of
Simon & Schuster, Inc.

For information about special discounts for bulk purchases, please contact Simon & Schuster Special Sales
at 1-866-506-1949 or business@simonandschuster.com.
The Simon & Schuster Speakers Bureau can bring authors to your live event. For more information or to
book an event contact the Simon & Schuster Speakers Bureau at 1-866-248-3049 or visit our website at
www.simonspeakers.com.
Manufactured in the United States of America 0518 LAK
2 4 6 8 10 9 7 5 3 1
Library of Congress Cataloging-in-Publication Data
Names: Williams, Bonnie, author. | McClurkan, Rob, illustrator.
Title: The secrets of Crayola's cool colors and hot hues / by Bonnie Williams; illustrated by Rob McClurkan.
Description: New York : Simon Spotlight, 2018. | Series: Science of fun stuff | Series: Ready-to-read | Audience:
Ages 6-8. | Audience: K to grade 3.
Identifiers: LCCN 2018002667 (print) | LCCN 2018002950 (ebook) | ISBN 9781534417755 (pbk) |
ISBN 9781534417762 (hc) | ISBN 9781534417779 (eBook)
Subjects: LCSH: Color—Juvenile literature. | Crayons—Juvenile literature. | Color vision—Juvenile literature. |
Crayola (Firm)—Juvenile literature.
Classification: LCC QC495.5 (ebook) | LCC QC495.5 .W557 2018 (print) | DDC 535.6—dc23
LC record available at https://lccn.loc.gov/2018002667

CONTENTS

CHAPTER 1
The Science Behind Crayons

Picture it. You have something in mind you'd like to draw. You take out a clean, unlined sheet of paper. You crack open the top of a box of Crayola crayons and see the flat points of the multicolored crayons, then smell that wonderful scent. You choose your first color, take the crayon out of the box, and make a smooth line of color on your paper.

Children around the world have been doing the same thing for well over 100 years since Crayola produced its first box of crayons in 1903. But how are Crayola crayons made? What ingredients are used to make them? And how do we even see color in the first place? By the end of this book you'll know the answers to these questions and more. You'll be a Science of Fun Stuff Expert on the colorful creation of crayons!

The magic starts with very pure paraffin wax and pigment. Paraffin wax is made from *petroleum*, an oil that comes from inside the earth. It does not have a color. So for crayons to be made, *pigment*— which is a fancy word for color—must be added. The pigment that Crayola uses comes in powdered form and is added to the melted wax. Today Crayola crayons come in 120 different colors.

Once the hot wax and colored powder have been mixed together, the liquid begins its journey through the factory assembly line. An *assembly line* is the order in which materials go through different machines or stations with workers to make a product. The colored wax is poured into crayon-shaped molds and cooled. It takes about five minutes for the crayons to cool. Then they are taken out of the molds and wrapped with labels. Each crayon is wrapped twice around with the label so that the crayon is extra

sturdy. Next the crayons get sorted by color. Once workers have inspected each crayon to make sure no points have been broken during this process, the perfect crayons are placed into boxes.

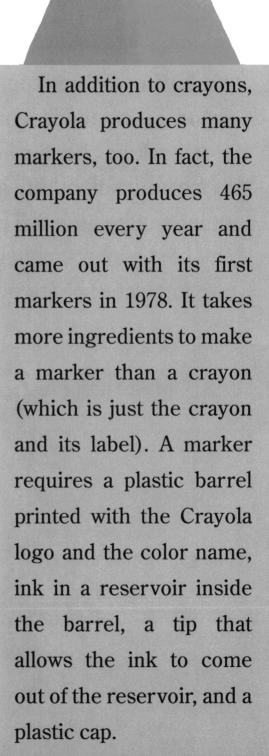

In addition to crayons, Crayola produces many markers, too. In fact, the company produces 465 million every year and came out with its first markers in 1978. It takes more ingredients to make a marker than a crayon (which is just the crayon and its label). A marker requires a plastic barrel printed with the Crayola logo and the color name, ink in a reservoir inside the barrel, a tip that allows the ink to come out of the reservoir, and a plastic cap.

Since 1988 Crayola has also made colored pencils. Today Crayola manufactures 600 million colored pencils each year. Colored pencils start with a wood casing made from trees. After the tree bark has been removed, the wood is treated, smoothed, and shaped so that color can be added. The color cores at the center of the pencils are created by mixing water, pigment, and extenders,

plus binding agents that hold everything together. This mixture is rolled out flat, then pressed into long, solid tube-like shapes called *cartridges*. Next they are cut into pencil-length pieces, dried, and placed on the wood. More wood is then added on top of the cartridge cores, and the two pieces of wood are glued tightly together. Then the wood is painted. Once the paint is dry, the pencils are sharpened and boxed up.

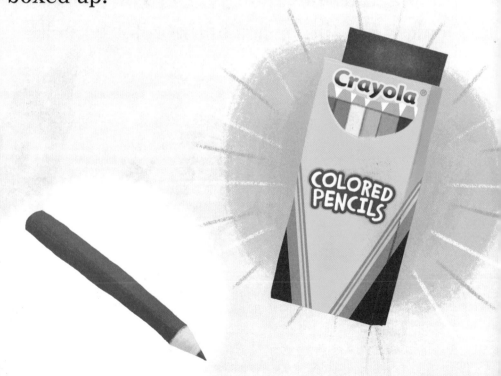

CHAPTER 2
Colorful Creations

So now that you know how these writing instruments are created, it's important that you understand how color is created. Life would be awfully dull if everything were black and white.

Crayola has 120 colors of crayons, and every single one of them is made from some combination of just three *primary colors*: red, blue, and yellow. The primary colors are the basics of the color wheel.

The next set of colors are known as *secondary colors*. They are made by a combination of equal parts red, yellow, or blue. So blue and red combined create violet. Blue and yellow combined create green. And yellow and red combined create orange.

By combining a primary and a secondary color, you create *tertiary colors.* So combining red and orange creates red-orange. Combining blue and green creates blue-green. Combining blue and violet creates blue-violet, and so on. Many different colors can be created from mixing primary and secondary colors depending on how much you mix in of one color over another color. Another way you could say that is that one color is the *dominant hue.* In other words, in yellow-green, there is more yellow than green, so yellow is the dominant hue.

If you look at the color wheel, you can easily see *complementary colors*. Complementary colors sit opposite each other on the color wheel. If you draw a straight line through the center of the circle from red, you hit green. If you draw a straight line from yellow, you hit violet. If you draw a straight line from blue, you hit orange. Complementary colors look great together, but sometimes they can be a little too strong and compete or vibrate against each other.

Another way to talk about color is the *temperature* of the color. Colors are either "cool" or "warm," although a color won't burn you or make you cold in real life. Rather, these terms refer to the feeling a

color evokes, or brings to mind. So reds, yellows, and oranges are considered warm colors. They are the colors of fire. Blues, greens, and violets are considered cool colors. They are the colors of the ocean.

There are still other ways to create colors. Adding white to any color will change its *tint*, making the color less saturated. Adding black to any color will change its *shade*, making the color more saturated. Adding a mixture of black and

white, or gray, adds *tone* to the original color. And, of course, you can add more or less white, black, or gray to create different color values. One way to think of color value is how dark or light the color is.

CHAPTER 3
See the Rainbow

Understanding a little about color theory, it's important to consider how we see color. We see color because of light. The sun's rays have wavelengths that we see as color. The colors human beings can see are those of the rainbow: red (the longest wavelength we can see), orange, yellow, green, blue, indigo, and violet (the shortest

wavelength we can see), as well as the colors in between those major hues. This is called the *visible spectrum*. Humans can see light that ranges from around 380 nanometers to 700 nanometers. (A *nanometer* is a very, very small unit of measurement.) When light hits an object, certain color wavelengths bounce back. So we see a red crayon because the red wavelengths in light are bouncing off of that crayon.

In order to see color, receptors in our eyes send information to our brains that then recognize the color. But there are many colors, or wavelengths, we can't see. They are outside a human being's visible spectrum. Longer wavelengths than red include infrared waves, microwaves, and radio waves. Shorter wavelengths than violet include ultraviolet light, X-rays, and gamma rays.

POW!

So far we have not discussed black and white, apart from adding them to other hues on the color wheel. What about those colors? Well, white reflects, or bounces back, all the wavelengths of

color, making it look colorless to us. Black absorbs, or takes in, all the wavelengths of color, making it look very dark. In fact, scientists who deal with color as light do not consider black to be a color at all!

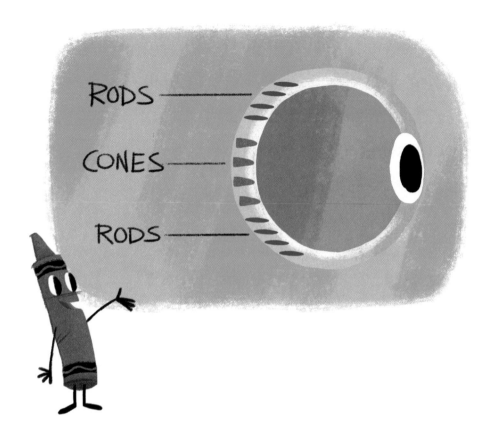

One more thing about the way we see
color as human beings: Some people are
color-blind, which means that they can't see
some colors. There are two kinds of cells in
our eyes that help us see color. *Rods* sense
light and darkness. *Cones* sense color.
Cones can sense reds, blues, and greens
and combinations of those three colors.

In someone who is color-blind, some of the cones don't work the way they do in other people. But not all people who are color-blind see things the same way. Some people can't see greens very well, and some people can't see blues very well. In very rare cases someone might not be able to see any color at all.

CHAPTER 4
Color Your World

Remember the temperature of colors? The mood a color evokes is just one of the ways color influences our world. In fact, color is so important that businesses often hire color consultants to give advice on designs for logos or even room decorations.

And it doesn't
stop there. People
are more likely to
buy a piece of fruit
that looks like the
color they have in
mind. The United
States Department
of Agriculture
even has standards
as to how each type of food should
look. So oranges should look classically
orange, there are measures for what color
different types of berries should be, and so
on. That's because taste doesn't depend on
just your taste buds and sense of smell. We
see what we eat too, and it can influence
how it tastes. It's kind of like when you
think you are about to drink a glass of
water and it turns out to be milk. The milk
tastes a little wrong because your brain
wasn't expecting it.

Like taste, color is also subjective, which means that the way you feel about a color has to do with your personal experience. For example, what is your favorite color? Why is that your favorite color? Do you have happy memories having to do with that color? Your next-door neighbor or best friend might feel differently about that color. They might associate happy feelings with another color.

You might also think of colors in certain ways because you've seen them associated that way for as long as you can remember. What do you think of when you see the colors orange and black together? Did you think of Halloween? Those colors have been used in Halloween decorations for a long time, and you probably see a lot of them every year during the month of October. But Halloween isn't celebrated in many other parts of the world, so when someone from another country sees orange and black together, they might have a completely different association.

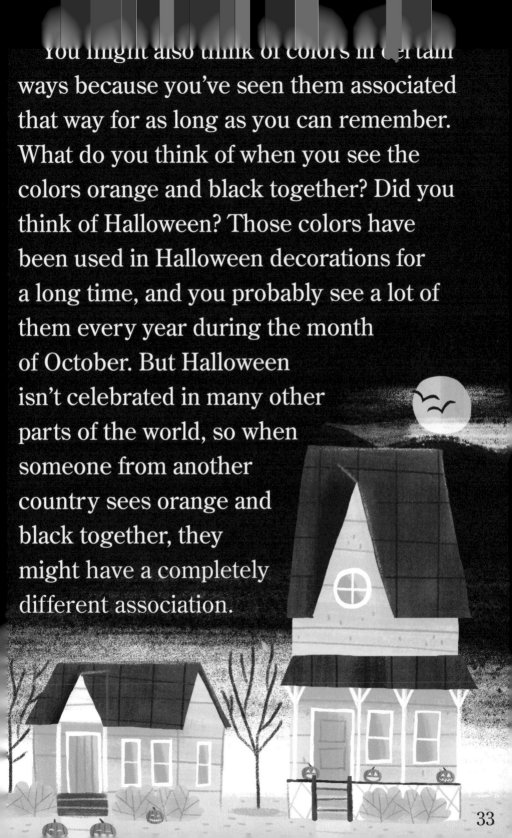

SCIENCE
OF FUN STUF
EXPERT

ON
CRAYON

Congratulations! You've reached the end of this book and are now an official Science of Fun Stuff expert on Crayola colors. So the next time you open a new box of Crayola crayons, remember all you know about how they are made and the colors they produce!

Hey, kids! Now that you're an expert on the science of Crayola colors, turn the page to get a sneak peek at what really happens behind the scenes at a Crayola crayon factory, learn how to perform a cool color experiment, and create your own color lab!

Behind the Scenes at Crayola

Each day many Crayola crayons are made. In fact, 8,500 crayons are made every minute in the main factory in

Easton, Pennsylvania. That's more than three billion per year!

Insta-rainbow

Would you like to make a rainbow? Here's what you'll need for this experiment:

- glass of water
- sheet of white paper
- flashlight

Fill the glass almost to the top with water. Place the glass of water on top of the sheet of paper.

Turn the flashlight on and shine it on the glass. You may need to move the flashlight a bit to get your rainbow to appear!

Create a Color Lab!

Would you like to set up your own color laboratory? Here's what you need to do so:

- red, yellow, and blue food coloring
- water
- 3 clear containers
- 3 eyedroppers
- clear plastic wrap
- sheet of white paper

Fill each container with water. Add three drops of food coloring into each container so that you have a batch of red, yellow, and blue.

Place the piece of clear plastic wrap on top of the white paper.

Using the eyedroppers, drop the different colors onto the plastic wrap and create some colors!

Being an expert on something means you can get an awesome score on a quiz on that subject! Take this

SCIENCE OF CRAYOLA QUIZ

to see how much you've learned.

1. Parrafin wax is made from:
   a. sugar
   b. petroleum
   c. ultraviolet waves

2. The primary colors are:
   a. red, white, blue
   b. red, yellow, black
   c. red, yellow, blue

3. Crayola produced its first box of crayons in:
   a. 1903
   b. 1978
   c. 2013

4. The complementary color for violet is:
   a. gray
   b. orange
   c. yellow

5. The cone cells in your eyes sense:
   a. temperature
   b. darkness
   c. color

6. How many markers does Crayola produce each year?
   a. 465 million
   b. 3 billion
   c. 285,000

7. Ultraviolet light, X-rays, and gamma rays have wavelengths that are:
   a. shorter than violet
   b. longer than red
   c. the same length as black

8. The dominant hue for blue-green is:
   a. green
   b. yellow
   c. blue

Answers: 1. b 2. c 3. a 4. c 5. c 6. a 7. a 8. c

REPRODUCIBLE